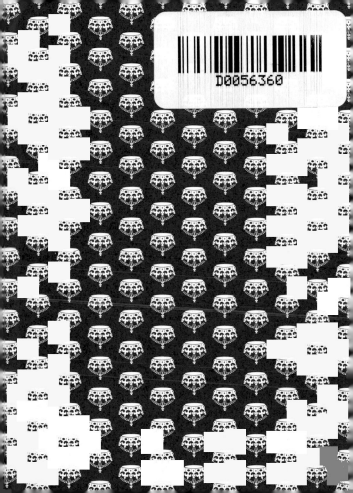

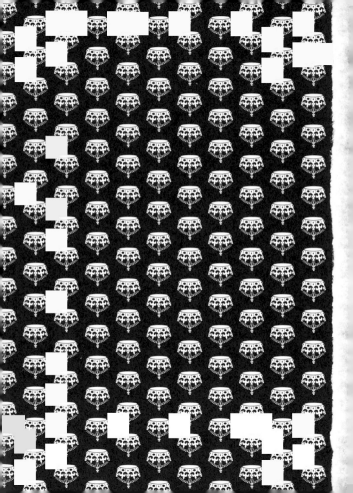

NOW
PANIC
AND
FREAK
OUT

Andrews McMeel Publishing, LLC
an Andrews McMeel Universal company
1130 Walnut Street, Kansas City, Missouri 64106

www.andrewsmcmeel.com

13 14 15 16 TEN 10 9 8 7 6 5

ISBN: 978-1-4494-1842-7

Library of Congress Control Number: 2011941254

Published by arrangement with Summersdale Publishers Ltd.

ATTENTION: SCHOOLS AND BUSINESSES
Andrews McMeel books are available at quantity discounts with bulk purchase for educational, business, or sales promotional use. For information, please e-mail the Andrews McMeel Publishing Special Sales Department: specialsales@amuniversal.com

NOW
PANIC
AND
FREAK
OUT

Andrews McMeel
Publishing, LLC

Kansas City • Sydney • London

When in danger or in doubt, run in circles, scream and shout.

Unknown

Anyone who isn't confused
really doesn't understand
the situation.

Edward R. Murrow

We experience moments
absolutely free from worry.
These brief respites are
called panic.

Cullen Hightower

We live in a
rainbow of chaos.

Paul Cézanne

Don't let aging get you down. It's too hard to get back up.

John Wagner

High-tech tomatoes.
Mysterious milk.
Supersquash. Are we
supposed to eat this stuff?
Or is it going to eat us?

Anita Manning

Every faculty . . . I possess
can be used as an
instrument with which to
worry myself.

Mark Rutherford

There's a fine line between genius and insanity. I have erased this line.

Oscar Levant

Try not to worry . . .
take each day just one
anxiety attack at
a time.

Tom Wilson

A question that sometimes drives me hazy: Am I or are the others crazy?

Albert Einstein

I don't want to retire.
I'm not that good at
crossword puzzles.

Norman Mailer

Love looks forward, hate looks back, anxiety has eyes all over its head.

Mignon McLaughlin

I think that was a
moment of cool
panic there.

Ron Atkinson

A word to the wise ain't
necessary—it's the stupid
ones that need the advice.

Bill Cosby

We are, perhaps, uniquely
among the earth's creatures,
the worrying animal.

Lewis Thomas

I accept chaos. I'm not sure whether it accepts me.

Bob Dylan

What sane person
could live in this world
and not be crazy?

Ursula K. Le Guin

It's nice to see that look of alarm on the faces of the others.

Graham Chapman

The reason why worry kills
more people than work is
that more people worry
than work.

Robert Frost

Exercise daily. Eat
wisely. Die anyway.

Anonymous

Don't worry that children
never listen to you; worry
that they are always
watching you.

Robert Fulghum

Life is not a spectacle
or a feast; it is a
predicament.

George Santayana

Laugh at yourself first,
before anyone
else can.

Elsa Maxwell

Dread of disaster makes
everybody act in the very
way that increases
the disaster.

Bertrand Russell

You have to go on and
be crazy. Craziness
is like heaven.

Jimi Hendrix

Every day I run scared.
That's the only way I can
stay ahead.

John H. Johnson

Better mad with the
rest of the world than
wise alone.

Baltasar Gracián

Leadership has been defined as the ability to hide your panic from others.

Anonymous

To live is so startling
it leaves little time for
anything else.

Emily Dickinson

The only thing to do with
good advice is to pass it on.
It is never of any use
to oneself.

Oscar Wilde

Speak when you're angry,
and you'll make the best
speech you'll ever regret.

Laurence J. Peter

When you become
senile, you won't
know it.

Bill Cosby

When one has too great a dread of what is impending, one feels some relief when the trouble has come.

Joseph Joubert

A zebra doesn't
change its spots.

Al Gore

Insanity is doing the
same thing over and
over again and expecting
different results.

Albert Einstein

Experience is a terrible teacher who sends horrific bills.

Anonymous

They couldn't hit
an elephant at this
distance.

Maj. Gen. John Sedgwick, just
before being shot and killed

I owe my success to having listened respectfully to the very best advice, and then going away and doing the exact opposite.

G. K. Chesterton

Do not take life too
seriously. You will
never get out of
it alive.

Elbert Hubbard

If crime went down
100 percent, it would still be
fifty times higher than it
should be.

John Bowman

Only one man ever understood me. And he didn't understand me.

G. W. F. Hegel

I used to believe that anything was better than nothing. Now I know that sometimes nothing is better.

Glenda Jackson

The only thing that
remains unsolved is
the resolution of
the problem.

Thomas Wells

Life is rather like a tin of sardines—we're all of us looking for the key.

Alan Bennett

If one synchronized
swimmer drowns, do all the
rest have to drown, too?

Steven Wright

Never worry about
your heart till it stops
beating.

E. B. White

The past is the
only dead thing that
smells sweet.

Edward Thomas

Moderation is a fatal thing.
Nothing succeeds
like excess.

Oscar Wilde

Make somebody
happy today. Mind
your own business.

Ann Landers

LIFE, n. A spiritual pickle
preserving the body
from decay.

Ambrose Bierce

Technological progress has merely provided us with more efficient means for going backwards.

Aldous Huxley

We live in an age when pizza gets to your home before the police.

Jeff Marder

In this world nothing can
be said to be certain,
except death and taxes.

Benjamin Franklin

The perfect normal
person is rare in
our civilization.

Karen Horney

It's all right letting yourself go, as long as you can let yourself back.

Mick Jagger

Insanity is hereditary. You get it from your children.

Sam Levenson

Life is a zoo in
a jungle.

Peter De Vries

I have a simple philosophy.
Fill what's empty, empty
what's full,and scratch
where it itches.

Alice Roosevelt Longworth

The future we're leaving
our children is less an
ecological legacy, more a
pre-emptive strike.

Rob Newman

If things go wrong,
don't go with them.

Roger Babson

Life is a roller coaster.
Try to eat a light
lunch.

David A. Schmaltz

Say what you will about the
Ten Commandments, you
must always come back to
the pleasant fact that there
are only ten of them.

H. L. Mencken

The difference between life and the movies is that a script has to make sense, and life doesn't.

Joseph L. Mankiewicz

Time you enjoy
wasting, was not
wasted.

John Lennon

Do not look where
you fell, but where
you slipped.

African proverb

Clothes make the man.
Naked people have little or
no influence in society.

Mark Twain

Most cars on our roads have only one occupant, usually the driver.

Carol Malia

I am free of all
prejudice. I hate
everyone equally.

W. C. Fields

Ah well! I am their
leader, I really had to
follow them!

Alexandre Auguste Ledru-Rollin

Experience was of no ethical value. It was merely the name men gave to their mistakes.

Oscar Wilde

God is good, but
never dance in a
small boat.

Irish proverb

We have to believe in
free will. We have
no choice.

Isaac Bashevis Singer

If history repeats itself, and
the unexpected always
happens, how incapable
must Man be of learning
from experience!

George Bernard Shaw

I've read about foreign policy and studied—
I know the number of continents.

George Wallace

Advice is what we ask for when we already know the answer but wish we didn't.

Erica Jong

Never saw off the
branch you are on,
unless you are being
hanged from it.

Stanislaw J. Lec

You want to run out in front,
prepare to be tripped
from behind.

S. A. Sachs

In the long run
we are all dead.

John Maynard Keynes

Don't ever take a
fence down until you
know the reason why
it was put up.

John F. Kennedy

I don't think you ever know in yourself whether you have gone mad.

Chris Lowe

Facts are stupid things.

Ronald Reagan

It only seems as if you are
doing something when
you're worrying.

Lucy Maud Montgomery

Life is the farce which everyone has to perform.

Arthur Rimbaud

The first half of our lives is ruined by our parents and the second half by our children.

Clarence Darrow

Multimedia? As far as I'm concerned, it's reading with the radio on.

Rory Bremner

Real difficulties can be overcome; it is only the imaginary ones that are unconquerable.

Theodore N. Vail

I hope life isn't a big
joke, because I
don't get it.

Jack Handey

If you haven't set off . . . yet,
the best thing to do is turn
back and go home.

Annie Nightingale

Science in the modern world
has many uses; its chief
use, however, is to provide
long words to cover the
errors of the rich.

G. K. Chesterton

Caution: cape does
not enable user to fly.

Warning label on a
Batman costume

I am an old man and
have known a great many
troubles, but most of them
never happened.

Mark Twain

Any idiot can face a
crisis—it's day to day
living that wears
you out.

Anton Chekhov

Not a shred of evidence
exists in favor of the idea
that life is serious.

Brendan Gill

Ignorance more
frequently begets
confidence than does
knowledge.

Charles Darwin

I've been absolutely terrified
every moment of my life.

Georgia O'Keeffe

Life is very interesting
if you make mistakes.

Georges Carpentier

Everything has been
figured out, except
how to live.

Jean-Paul Sartre

There was never yet an uninteresting life. Such a thing is an impossibility. Inside of the dullest exterior there is a drama, a comedy, and a tragedy.

Mark Twain

China is a big
country, inhabited by
many Chinese.

Charles de Gaulle

If the world should blow
itself up, the last audible
voice would be that of an
expert saying it can't
be done.

Peter Ustinov

And in the end, it's not the years in your life that count. It's the life in your years.

Abraham Lincoln

Real life seems
to have no plots.

Ivy Compton-Burnett

If Lincoln were alive today, he'd roll over in his grave.

Gerald Ford

I have opinions of my own,
strong opinions, but I don't
always agree with them.

George H. W. Bush

Life is one fool thing after another whereas love is two fool things after each other.

Oscar Wilde

Life is divided into the horrible and the miserable.

Woody Allen

For peace of mind, we
need to resign as general
manager of the universe.

Larry Eisenberg

Thanks be to God,
I am still an atheist.

Luis Buñuel

Suicide is a real threat to health in a modern society.

Virginia Bottomley

I have left orders to be awakened at any time in case of national emergency, even if I'm in a Cabinet meeting.

Ronald Reagan

We've got to pause and ask
ourselves: How much clean
air do we need?

Lee Iacocca

The art of life is more like the wrestler's art than the dancer's.

Marcus Aurelius

The time to begin most
things is ten years ago.

Mignon McLaughlin

The purpose of life is
to fight maturity.

Dick Werthimer

The tide is very much
in our court now.

Kevin Keegan

Experience is a comb that
life gives you after you
lose your hair.

Judith Stern

I used to eat a lot of natural
foods until I learned that
most people die of
natural causes.

Anonymous

All life is an experiment.

Ralph Waldo Emerson

Rowe's Rule: the odds
are five to six that the light
at the end of the tunnel
is the headlight of
an oncoming train.

Paul Dickson

In the Soviet army, it takes more courage to retreat than advance.

Joseph Stalin

(Osama Bin Laden is)
either alive and well,
or alive and not well,
or not alive.

Donald Rumsfeld

It is true what Philosophy says: that Life must be understood backwards. But that makes one forget the other saying: that it must be lived—forwards.

Søren Kierkegaard

I love deadlines. I like the
whooshing noise they make
as they go by.

Douglas Adams

When things are perfect, that's when you need to worry most.

Drew Barrymore

If we weren't all crazy,
we'd just go insane.

Jimmy Buffett

When one subtracts from
life infancy (which is
vegetation),—sleep, eating,
and swilling—buttoning
and unbuttoning—how
much remains of downright
existence? The summer
of a dormouse.

Lord Byron

Hard work never killed
anybody, but why
take a chance?

Edgar Bergen

I never put off till tomorrow
what I can possibly do . . .
the day after.

Oscar Wilde

Death is one of the
few things that can
be done as easily
lying down.

Woody Allen

It may be that your sole
purpose in life is simply to
serve as a warning
to others.

Unknown

Just because nobody
complains doesn't mean all
parachutes are perfect.

Benny Hill

The trouble with the
rat race is that even if
you win you're still
a rat.

Lily Tomlin

Life is a horizontal fall.

Jean Cocteau

Constantly choosing the lesser of two evils is still choosing evil.

Jerry Garcia

We're not retreating,
we're just advancing in a
different direction.

Maj. Gen. Oliver P. Smith

They
misunderestimated
me.

George W. Bush

To lose one parent . . .
may be regarded as a
misfortune; to lose both
looks like carelessness.

Oscar Wilde

I don't suffer from insanity. I enjoy every minute of it.

Anonymous

You know, solving other
people's problems is easy.
The only person I can't
seem to figure out is myself.

Thomas James Higgins

You're only given
a little spark of
madness. You mustn't
lose it.

Robin Williams

That's the problem with living in continual chaos. It's exhausting, sometimes frightening, like riding on a roller coaster blindfolded. The catch is that it's also very exciting and very addictive.

Lorna Luft

In a mad world,
only the mad
are sane.

Akira Kurosawa

My experience is that as soon as people are old enough to know better, they don't know anything at all.

Oscar Wilde

The Tory Party only
panics in a crisis.

Iain Macleod

Correct me if I'm wrong, but hasn't the fine line between sanity and madness gotten finer?

George Price

Only two things are infinite,
the universe and human
stupidity, and I'm not sure
about the former.

Albert Einstein

Forget the past—
the future will give you
plenty to worry about.

George Allen Sr.

Be careful about reading
health books. You may die
of a misprint.

Mark Twain

The email of the species is more deadly than the mail.

Stephen Fry

The people who know how to run the country are busy driving taxicabs and cutting hair.

George Burns

The man who smiles
when things go
wrong has thought of
someone to blame
it on.

Robert Bloch

Time, time—that is our greatest master! Alas, like Ugolino, time devours its own children.

Hector Berlioz

Most accidents occur within
five minutes of the home.
Move house.

Milton Berle

Life isn't fair.
It's just fairer than
death, that's all.

William Goldman